COASTAL LIVING®

outdoor spaces

COASTAL LIVING®

outdoor spaces

*Fresh Ideas for Stylish Porches,
Decks, Patios & Gardens*

Oxmoor House®

ISBN 13: 978-0-8487-3913-3
ISBN 10: 0-8487-3913-2
Library of Congress Control Number: 2013930444

Printed in the United States of America
First Printing 2013

OXMOOR HOUSE

Editorial Director: **Leah McLaughlin**
Creative Director: **Felicity Keane**
Brand Manager: **Fonda Hitchcock**
Senior Editor: **Heather Averett**
Managing Editor: **Rebecca Benton**

For more books to enrich your life, visit oxmoorhouse.com.

PHOTOGRAPHY CREDITS

Front Cover: Tria Giovan
Back Cover: Miki Duisterhof (top), Jonny Valiant (middle), Lynn Karlin (bottom)
Inside Flap: Tria Giovan

COASTAL LIVING® OUTDOOR SPACES

Art Director: **Claire Cormany**
Project Editor: **Megan McSwain Yeatts**
Senior Production Manager: **Susan Chodakiewicz**
Production Manager: **Theresa Beste-Farley**

CONTRIBUTORS

Editor: **Steele Thomas Marcoux**
Designer: **Carol O. Loria**
Photography Editor: **Philippine Scali**
Copy Editors: **Donna Baldone, Lauren Brooks**
Proofreaders: **Stephanie Gibson, Polly Linthicum**
Indexer: **Mary Ann Laurens**
Interns: **Megan Branagh, Frances Gunnells, Susan Kemp, Sara Lyon, Staley McIlwain, Jeffrey Preis, Maria Sanders, Julia Sayers**

COASTAL LIVING®

Editor-In-Chief: **Antonia van der Meer**
Design Director: **Victor Maze**
Executive Editor: **Jennifer Brunnemer Slaton**
Managing Editor: **Amy Lowe Mitchell**
Style Director: **Linda Hirst**
Homes Editor: **Brielle M. Ferreira**
Assistant Lifestyle & Beauty Editor: **Amber Furst**
Senior Editor, Food: **Julia Rutland**
Travel Editor: **Jacquelyne Froeber**
Associate Features Editor: **Marisa Spyker**
Editor-at-Large: **Erin Swift**

ART

Deputy Art Director: **Tempy Segrest**
Designer: **Brittany Kenny**
Associate Photo Editor: **Kristen Shelton Fielder**

COPY

Copy Chief: **Katie Finley**

PRODUCTION

Production Manager: **Jamie Barnhart**
Copy/Production Associate: **Caitlin Murphree Miller**

EDITORIAL SUPPORT

Office Manager: **Mamie Walling**

TIME HOME ENTERTAINMENT INC.

Publisher: **Jim Childs**
VP, Strategy & Business Development: **Steven Sandonato**
Executive Director, Marketing Services: **Carol Pittard**
Executive Director, Retail & Special Sales: **Tom Mifsud**
Director, Bookazine Development & Marketing: **Laura Adam**
Executive Publishing Director: **Joy Butts**
Associate Publishing Director: **Megan Pearlman**
Finance Director: **Glenn Buonocore**
Associate General Counsel: **Helen Wan**

Sometimes, what's on the outside does matter most—

especially at the coast. From extending a warm welcome with a cheerful entry to encouraging exploration in a garden, outdoor spaces provide the setting for many of our most cherished moments with friends and family—and they offer opportunities to pause and unplug from the indoor world's harried pace.

Here, we've gathered beautiful outdoor living spaces, from gorgeous gardens that could turn even a couch potato into a nature enthusiast to seaside-inspired paint picks, maintenance tips, and more. So take a seat, dive in, and start making plans to live life outside.

CONTENTS

outdoor living

gardening

planning

outdoor living

At the beach, family memories are made outside. Whether you're preparing a meal on the grill, cooling off in the pool, playing board games on a porch with an ocean view, or watching sunsets on the dock, outdoor living spaces are the activity hubs of coastal homes. Designing these areas presents unique challenges—from weatherproofing to heavy-duty material selection—but they also offer opportunities to infuse your home with a vacation vibe. The inspiring ideas on the pages that follow will help you combine practicality with easy, breezy panache in your outdoor space, whether you live on the coast or just love seaside style.

1

ENTRIES & EXTERIORS

A house makes its first impression with its front door and facade, which convey to guests a sense of the personality and style inside (and thus a little something about the owners, too). Here's great news: This is one first impression that you can do over. Exterior makeovers can be as simple as changing out paint colors and adding window boxes, and they often can be completed in a single day. So pick a new palette, a few great light fixtures, and some sweet little extras like iron house numbers or a nautical doorknocker, and your home will be brimming with curb appeal in a snap.

refined welcome

A careful balance of light and dark and casual and formal elements adds subtle drama to the entry of this Dutch Colonial home.

PAINTED ELEMENTS

Dark gray-brown paint in a semigloss finish highlights the entry's distinctive architecture, such as the deep, overhanging eave supported by long brackets and the wide trim around the door and windows.

DUTCH DOOR

Also known as a stable door, split doors like this one maintain privacy and provide protection while ushering in sunshine and gentle breezes. This is a project you shouldn't tackle yourself; instead, ask the door manufacturer to recommend contractors in your area who are familiar with hanging your particular model.

SYMMETRICAL SEATING

Simple teak benches placed on either side of the front door take on an unexpected air of sophistication thanks to their plush custom cushions and outdoor throw pillows.

— *Material Matters* —

Downspouts made of copper are extremely sturdy and will not corrode, develop holes, or come apart. Over time, they develop a natural patina that will change their shiny, brassy finish to a more muted brown-green shade. Copper downspouts are more expensive than other options, but if properly installed, they should last the lifetime of the house.

Steal This Idea
Install hook-and-eye hardware that will hold open doors to cool your house with cross breezes.

island aloha

Doors and shutters painted the same color as the Caribbean Sea give this tropical villa's entry local flavor.

TURQUOISE ACCENTS
If you opt for a bright front door color like this one, skip a glossy paint finish and go for eggshell or flat instead so it isn't too intense. Stick with neutral shades elsewhere (such as on the siding and trim) to let the bold entry be the star of the show.

LOCAL VEGETATION
This potted citrus tree lends tropical flair to the entrance. Thanks to the temperate climate, the hardy plant will thrive outside year-round with minimal maintenance. Bonus: The fruit brings a pop of vibrant color and a fragrant scent to the entry.

HERRINGBONE STOOP
Large terra-cotta tiles laid in a herringbone pattern up the fun factor outside this front door. This kind of clay flooring is a smart choice for tropical locales because it can withstand the heat.

Material Matters
In coastal or other high-moisture climates, installing marine-quality door hardware with a finish that will not corrode or rust is essential. Oil-rubbed bronze or stainless steel are attractive options.

all-american abode

Traditional architecture, a blue-and-white scheme, and a few patriotic pops of red infuse this shingle-style house with timeless appeal.

CLASSIC PALETTE

The home's Nantucket-style architecture gets a bit of added interest thanks to its clever use of color. The doors and decorative shutters are painted a deep navy, which looks crisp and elegant against the silver-gray tone of the patinated cedar shingles. Bright pinks, reds, and purples from the surrounding landscape also contribute to the home's fresh-faced charm.

WELL-PLACED LIGHTING

Exterior fixtures need not be limited to illuminating the front door. Here, sconces mounted between second-story windows and a lantern fixed atop a post along the entry path give off an inviting glow.

CEDAR-SHAKE SIDING

This home's shingled siding is a wise choice at the coast, where the wood's natural insect- and water-repellent qualities add a functional purpose to the decorative look. Despite their hardiness, cedar-shake shingles must be routinely treated with a sealant to bolster protection against rot and mildew. Keep in mind that new shingles will have a golden color that will turn gray with time.

california cool

Traditional elements like board-and-batten siding and boxwood shrubs get fresh updates to give a beach bungalow a modern twist.

ALL-OVER PAINT
Painting every surface, from the shutters and garage door to the siding and front balconies, the same shade gives the architectural elements a more contemporary feel. The homeowners picked the hue because it resembles the color of weathered driftwood.

STEP IT UP
Want to bring your front door to new heights? Why not do it literally? Make a second-floor entry sing by building an extra-wide staircase with an unusual shape and then dressing it up with potted plants.

TRAILING VINES
It's good to embrace a little romance, even in the most contemporary homes. Here, climbing vines soften the straight, clean lines of the architecture.

modern cottage

A flat roof, single-pane windows and doors, and a general lack of adornment give this compact house a sleek look.

MATERIAL VARIETY

Who says a house has to have only one kind of siding? Here, three different materials—vertical cedar planks on the garage, guest room, and kitchen wing; blue cement panels on the entry, stairwell, and upstairs study wing; and horizontal cedar planks on the living space and master bed and bath wing—define separate areas of the house.

ALUMINUM FRAMES

The metal casing on the doors and windows not only provides slick contrast to the cedar planking but also offers greater insulation to better resist the elements.

PEA GRAVEL DRIVEWAY

The home's pea gravel driveway makes for a charming alternative to the more traditional black asphalt. Because it's permeable, the gravel cuts down on water runoff; plus you can hear visitors coming before they ring the doorbell.

rustic hideaway

Reclaimed wood with a weathered finish, antique doors with patina, and surfaces with gritty texture make this brand new house look like it's been there forever.

SALVAGED COLUMNS

Peeled-timber logs stand in for columns on this French Creole-inspired porch. The weathered wood echoes the gray-brown color of the front door and adds character to the new building.

ANTIQUE DOORS

The distressed finish of the 19th-century oak front door juxtaposed with the slick, industrial look of the vintage iron-and-glass French doors creates textural contrast on the house's portico.

VERDANT LANDSCAPING

Lush plantings like soft grass and spiky succulents bring an organic, lively touch to the otherwise somber setting. Planters made of materials used on the exterior—such as concrete, stone, and metal—tie the style of the garden to that of the house.

— *Material Matters* —

When used as siding, stucco (which is made of cement, sand, lime, and water) is an extremely durable, fire-resistant, low-maintenance material. It's also a great insulator of warm and cool air, and can be custom colored and textured to suit your aesthetic. Stucco does get dirty easily, so plan on spraying down your walls seasonally with a hose (a pressure-washer can cause damage). Be sure to inspect it regularly for cracks, which will need to be patched before they widen.

PULL IT TOGETHER

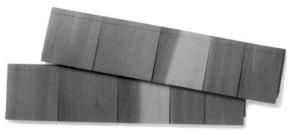

CHOOSE…
siding

All siding materials come with pros and cons—and there is no such thing as maintenance-free siding. When making your choice, consider the style of your house and your climate. For example, stucco is a smart option in the Southwest because of its heat tolerance and strong insulating capacities, while cedar shingles or planking, which are naturally resistant to moisture, make sense in the Pacific Northwest and New England. Thanks to its insulating quality and moisture tolerance, brick is frequently used in the Midwest and Southeast. Last but not least, engineered siding materials like board-formed concrete or cement panels are a more durable alternative to traditional wood clapboards.

CONSIDER ADDING…
shutters

Shutters are a great way to add architectural interest to your home's facade. Keep in mind that every shutter on your house need not be the same size; all that matters is that each shutter properly fits its adjacent window. There's a wide variety of styles from which to choose: awning, or Bermuda, shutters that hinge from the top of a window and are held open with rods; traditional louvered or paneled shutters that hinge on the sides and are held open with shutterdogs; or flat, planked shutters that feature decorative cutouts.

EXTEND A WARM WELCOME WITH…
lighting

When it comes to exterior lighting, think beyond your front door. Fixtures can serve either to highlight significant features of your home, such as beautiful windows or landscaping, or to illuminate alternative entry points, like garages or pathways. Gas or electric fixtures provide consistent, reliable light, while candlelit fixtures cast a softer glow.

BOOST CURB APPEAL WITH…
landscaping

From beautiful hedges to colorful beds of annuals and perennials, there's no better way to say "welcome home" than with well-manicured plantings. If you don't have a green thumb, fear not! Just choose a species of evergreen shrub that thrives in your climate.

2
PORCHES & LOGGIAS

When asked to imagine the most relaxing spot on Earth, many people dream of a porch with a hammock or rocking chair, cool breezes, and a stunning view. As transition spaces between indoors and out, porches and loggias (open-air, gallery-style rooms accessible from the inside) can be furnished with all the coziness of interior living rooms. This chapter will show you how to transform these areas into the perfect places to unwind while taking in the scenery.

Steal This Idea

For a layered look and extra soft feel, pile a patterned rug, like this indoor/outdoor striped one, on top of a woven natural fiber rug, like this sea grass one.

polished ease

The generous proportions of this seaside porch make room for dining and living areas that look right at home with the house's classical architectural details.

FULLY FURNISHED

With a large dining table, sofas, chairs, side tables, rugs, and even lamps, this beachfront porch feels almost as polished as an indoor room. The only real difference between the two is that, from the iron and stone tables to the synthetic wicker seating, most of the furniture is resistant to moisture. Pieces that are not, like the lamp, can be stored inside when the space is not in use.

HANGING LANTERN

This custom-designed copper lantern has oxidized from exposure to the salty coastal air, giving it a green patina that adds character to the newly built porch. To prevent oxidation and preserve copper's shiny, brassy finish, treat surfaces with a clear protective polymer coating, available at hardware stores.

ARCHITECTURAL DETAILS

Classical elements such as the fluted columns, Greek key trim, and coffered ceiling help this second-story porch feel like a true extension of the house's formal interiors, which boast similar design features.

Material Matters

If you're in love with wicker but want to be able to leave your porch furniture out year-round, here's some good news: Plenty of manufacturers now make all-weather pieces that look as good as the real thing. Constructed from a synthetic material woven around an aluminum frame, these pieces are lightweight and breathable, just like traditional wicker. If you still prefer the classic stuff, keep it painted and sealed (with a clear marine varnish) during the summer and plan on bringing it inside during the winter months.

bold gesture

This porch combines classic shingle-style cottage architecture and wicker furnishings with striking graphic upholstery and a glossy red floor for a daring twist on tradition.

WICKER ROCKERS

Like cream and coffee, eggs and bacon, and peanut butter and jelly, front porches and wicker rocking chairs are a perfect pair—it's hard to imagine one without the other. Just because the combo is expected, however, doesn't mean you can't get creative. A coat of black paint gives typical rockers a more modern silhouette.

BLACK AND WHITE

The swan paintings and cabana-striped cushions bring graphic pattern to this porch. Although the color duo is strong, it's not out of context: The homeowner picked the palette for the furnishings based on the paint colors on the shutters and trim to ensure the design was cohesive.

PAINTED FLOOR

Painting your porch floor fiery red with a high-gloss finish takes courage. But here's why it works: All of the other colors on the porch are neutrals, and all of the other paint finishes are either semigloss or flat, which provide contrast to the bright and shiny floor.

screen saver

A mix of furniture styles and materials, a lively color scheme, and a pile of printed pillows create a laid-back feel on this screened porch.

PAINTED CEILING
Porch ceilings were traditionally painted sky blue for a host of anecdotal purposes, ranging from keeping evil spirits away to staving off bugs. Here, the soft shade in a semigloss finish adds airy contrast to the richness of the magenta and brown.

PRETTY PILLOWS
Solid upholstery plus a variety of printed pillows is a no-fail sofa strategy, inside or out. Here, bold piping on the sofa cushions in a hue pulled from the pillow fabric lends a cohesive touch. Bonus: Pillows are easy to swap out when you want a change.

RESIN LAMP
This white faux bois floor lamp is not only much lighter than its real wood counterparts, but it also can stay outside in all weather conditions. (The shade, however, should be brought indoors when the porch is not in use for long periods of time.)

—— *Material Matters* ——

If you live in an area plagued by mosquitoes, consider screening your porch so you can enjoy the outdoors. There are a variety of screen options on the market: aluminum (the most common; available in charcoal, silver, or black); fiberglass (resistant to shrinking and corrosion); bronze and copper (which hold up well in seaside areas but have a finish that will patina with time); epoxy-coated or stainless steel (another smart choice for seaside areas); and vinyl-coated polyester (stronger than typical screens, making it a good option for low panels, where pets and small children might come into contact with it).

sleeping beauty

Outfitted with cushy hanging beds, this screened porch is set up for long naps and sweet dreams.

HANGING DAYBEDS
These extra-deep blue swings are fitted with twin mattresses decked out in custom-made ticking stripe covers. Square and bolster pillows create a soft spot to hang with friends but can be easily removed for siestas.

BREEZY FANS
A pair of ceiling fans ensures that surroundings stay cool and comfortable when the breezes die down. Another idea: Keep a pair of tabletop fans stored away and bring them out when needed.

FLOOR-LENGTH DRAPES
Made of water- and fade-resistant fabric, these curtains not only bring soft texture and privacy to the space but also block the sun's bright glare, cooling the porch down on super hot days. During cooler seasons, the curtains can be drawn to trap heat inside.

Steal This Idea

Paint trim a nature-inspired shade like this sea green to give screened walls definition. This designer trick is a great way to add color to a neutral outdoor space like this one.

laid-back living

Bare floors, a soft hammock, and a collection of Adirondack chairs lend a simple, casual feel to this island villa porch.

ADIRONDACK CHAIRS

Their sit-down, stay-a-while style makes these super comfy seats perfect for a cozy porch. In a covered area, painted wood chairs can be easily maintained with routine wipe downs and a fresh coat of paint every few years. For less sheltered spots, such as decks, consider synthetic, weather-resistant versions instead. Bonus: Adirondack chairs have wide, flat arms that are great for setting a drink on—so you don't need a table.

HANGING HAMMOCK

To avoid telltale rope marks on your skin while you nap, opt for a quilted, cotton version, which is much softer than woven varieties.

OUTDOOR ARTWORK

Canvas paintings hung on the house's exterior walls add color and personality. Thanks to the roof's deep eaves, the paintings are sheltered from afternoon rain showers but need to be stored inside during strong storms. Painted ceramic pieces are also well suited for outdoor display.

resort chic

On this porch, gauzy drapes and loungey seating, like these daybeds and floor cushions, conjure the relaxed-but-stylish vibe of swanky hotel pool decks.

SHEER CURTAINS
These extra-long versions attached by simple grommets filter harsh sunlight, add soft texture, and lend a far-flung, tropical air to the porch.

MINIMALIST DAYBEDS
The streamlined frames and simple cushions have a clean, modern aesthetic and are surprisingly comfortable. Another plus: They're lightweight, which makes reconfiguring them for a party a breeze.

LACQUERED TABLES
The high-gloss paint finish of these red side tables contains polyurethane, which provides a hint of glint and also protects the pieces from exposure to heat and moisture.

old world

This poolside loggia's heavily textured natural materials, traditional architectural details, and rich colors are reminiscent of a Renaissance-era Tuscan villa.

WEATHERPROOF WICKER
Because this loggia is slightly more exposed to rain and moisture than most porches due to its ground-level location, the homeowners decided to forgo natural wicker furniture in favor of a copycat synthetic version that is made to withstand water and UV rays. Throw pillows in garnet and turquoise complement the chocolate brown frames and taupe cushions.

COFFERED CEILING
The ceiling's geometric configuration highlights the contrast between the smooth plaster recesses and rough-hewn beams, infusing the loggia with texture, pattern, and romantic sophistication.

STONE FLOORS
Celebrated for their durability, stone floors are great for covered outdoor spaces like this one. They can withstand tons of foot traffic and exposure to the elements, and they're easily cleaned with a simple hose down.

coastal tradition

A striped rug, rattan furniture, and blue cushions and pillows give this loggia a smart seaside scheme.

ALUMINUM RATTAN
The ornate frames and careful detailing of this sofa, pair of armchairs, and coffee table are proof positive that all-weather rattan (made of a synthetic fiber woven around an aluminum frame) is just as attractive as the natural version.

INDOOR/OUTDOOR RUG
This striped, woven polypropylene area rug is soft and pretty enough for indoor use but can withstand exposure to moisture and UV rays, too. The best part: Spills are easy to clean up—just soak them with a hose, and let the rug air-dry in the sun.

POTTED PLANTS
Palms and fiddle leaf fig trees look lovely on the covered loggia. For a seamless look, choose plant varieties and pots that complement the style of your garden and home.

— *Material Matters* —

Brick floors work well in loggias because they're durable and easy to maintain. New bricks are relatively inexpensive; salvaged bricks, which cost a little more, have a less standard, more varied feel and add character.

PULL IT TOGETHER

MAKE A SMART CHOICE WITH…
a painted floor

Porch floors that are constructed from wood must be protected from moisture by either a clear sealant or paint, which provides an opportunity to incorporate color and even pattern into your outdoor area. Choose a color that complements the exterior palette of your house. As for patterns, checkerboards and stripes are classic but anything you can dream up—and mark off with painter's tape or design with stencils—is fair game. The key to creating a professional-looking finish is all in the prep work: A previously painted porch floor must be sanded smooth before it can be primed. After that, apply two coats of porch-and-floor paint formulated with polyurethane that will protect surfaces from scuffs, dirt, moisture, and sunlight. For an extra-glossy finish, use metal-and-wood enamel.

KICK BACK IN…
rockers, hammocks, and swings

A porch almost wouldn't be a porch without some sort of seating that allows you to swing or sway a little. There's just something about the gentle movement that creates instant calm. Rocking chairs and hammocks come in a wide variety of styles and materials, and swings can be custom built to accommodate cushions as large as a twin mattress, if you want them to double as daybeds.

LIGHT IT UP WITH…
lanterns

Whether mounted from the ceiling and powered by gas or electricity or set atop tables or on the floor and illuminated with candles, lantern-style lighting casts just the right amount of glow to infuse any porch with a welcoming vibe. Depending on your decor, look for traditional carriage or nautical lanterns in bronze or brass; sleek, nickel-plated lanterns with a contemporary edge; or pierced-metal versions with bohemian flair.

COOL IT OFF WITH…
ceiling fans

One way to guarantee you'll use your porch more often, especially during the summer months, is to keep it cool with ceiling fans. It doesn't matter if your porch has a traditional, beachy, rustic, or modern look, there's a ceiling fan to suit your style.

3
PAVILIONS, PERGOLAS & GAZEBOS

Take advantage of beach scenery—or mild climates—with an outdoor living room. The space you choose depends on how you plan to use it: Pavilions (covered, open-air rooms under their own roofs but sometimes attached to a house) typically function as an extension of the home's interior; pergolas (freestanding post-and-beam structures) are simpler and less formal; and gazebos (stand-alone structures) offer a destination feel. These gathering places will make you want to live everyday life outdoors.

natural wonder

Rattan seating, floral fabrics, raffia pillows, and a rush rug feel right at home in the tropical, open-air setting of this formal pavilion.

RATTAN FURNITURE

For patio furniture with an organic look and high durability, seek out pieces made from rattan. When treated with a sealant, the durable, organic material can withstand the high heat, wind, and occasional rain of tropical climates. (In temperate climates, rattan furniture should not be left outside year-round.)

RUSH RUG

Woven rugs made of strong grasses blend in seamlessly outside and soften the surface of hardscaping, giving the space a true living room feel. Prolonged exposure to moisture will cause them to deteriorate over time, however, so consider storing them indoors when not in use.

CLASSIC ARCHITECTURE

Vaulted ceilings and lattice screens give the free-standing structure a feeling of permanence and provide a more formal setting for poolside parties.

soft spot

Draped in outdoor curtains and piled high with pillows, the bench in this gazebo is a cozy spot to lounge with friends or curl up with a book.

WEATHERPROOF CURTAINS
Made of water- and fade-resistant fabric, these curtain panels shield the gazebo from the sun and prying eyes. When installing outdoor drapes, look for marine-quality rods and rings that won't rust or corrode when exposed to moisture.

BUILT-IN BANQUETTE
Topped with plush cushions upholstered in durable outdoor fabric, this wraparound bench can accommodate a crowd for predinner appetizers and post-dinner cocktails.

METAL LANTERN
Outfit hanging fixtures with a low-wattage bulb to create warm ambience without overwhelming the space with a bright glare. The pierced pattern on this oil-rubbed bronze lantern casts dramatic shadows on the gazebo's roof.

——— *Material Matters* ———

Outdoor fabrics that can endure exposure to water and sun are a great solution for creating inviting and durable living spaces that make you want to linger outside. To ensure your cushions and pillows are resistant to rot, you need all-weather inserts made of acrylic fill and a polypropylene cover, as well.

bare minimum

Made of tree trunks and outfitted with just the essentials, this pergola demonstrates an easy-breezy understanding of island life.

SIMPLE CONSTRUCTION
There's no need for formality when the beach is your backyard. Here, the homeowners stuck to the basics, erecting a simple roof held up by slender tree trunks to provide just enough shade for the downtime between their swims.

OPEN ROOF
The pergola's roof was built from the loosely woven trunks of young blue gum trees (a variety of eucalyptus), which are extremely durable and resistant to fading in the sun. Bonus: This species is sustainably harvested.

FULLY FURNISHED
Despite the lack of armchairs or lounge chairs, this pergola has spots for sitting, lounging, and eating. All it takes is a built-in bench, a hammock, and a dining table and chairs to create the perfect spot for a respite—though the view doesn't hurt. Large throw pillows help soften the space.

louver's lane

With all-weather furniture, a soft and stylish rug, and operable louvered shutters that help modulate the breezes, this gazebo has all the comforts of indoor living.

WIND CONTROL

Outside spaces near the sea switch from too windy to too humid from one moment to the next. These louvered shutters can direct a mild-to-medium breeze or provide protection from stronger gusts.

TEAK FURNITURE

Thanks to oil in the trunks of its trees, teak is a naturally water-resistant wood and a smart, long-lasting option for outdoor furniture. Periodic treatment with teak oil, available at any home goods or hardware store, will help preserve its water resistance for years to come.

CONVERSATION SEATING

Take a cue from geometry and furnish a square space with circular seating arrangements. Four chairs sitting around a coffee table and rug will facilitate conversation—and, in an open-air room like this, ensure each person has a window seat.

rustic warmth

This picnic pavilion's cedar-and-stone construction and giant fireplace embody earthy style.

SALVAGED TIMBERS
Made of unused lumber from the owners' main house, this pavilion makes the most of precious building materials. The rough-hewn timbers and simple post-and-beam construction lend rustic charm.

STONE HEARTH
Nothing draws a crowd like an outdoor fireplace. Because they're a source of light and heat, fireplaces can make stand-alone structures suitable for use all day—and all year.

METAL ROOF
They don't shrink or erode with long-term exposure to sunlight and moisture, so metal roofs last much longer than traditional shingled versions (up to 50 years!). They also reflect a lot of heat from the sun, which helps keep the space below cooler, thereby reducing energy consumption. Look for a zinc or zinc-aluminum coating to prevent rust.

four-seasons room

Surrounded by floor-to-ceiling, shutter-clad openings and outfitted with a fireplace and cool tile floor, this pavilion is fully equipped for year-round (and all-weather) comfort.

FOOT REST

This handsome ottoman does double duty, acting as the ideal landing pad for drinks and treats when friends are visiting.

TILED FLOOR

No need for a rug when you have a barefoot-friendly tiled floor as pretty as this. The smooth surface is super low-maintenance: It can endure extreme heat and tons of moisture, and a spray-down with a hose will clean up sand or spills.

STOCKED BAR

A prep sink, countertop, mini-fridge, and storage cabinet prevent trips back to the kitchen when someone's cocktail needs refreshing.

Steal This Idea

These stacked ceramic fireballs (which require a gas burner) provide as much heat as typical gas logs and look chic when not in use.

garden getaway

A stone path meanders through thick foliage and delicate flowers to this vine-covered, stone-and-cedar gazebo that epitomizes romance.

CEDAR-SHAKE ROOF

With its weathered gray-brown color and rough look, the gazebo's cedar-shake roof is a natural fit for this garden gathering spot. Though this material is extremely resistant to wind and moisture, it must be treated with a sealant to protect against mildew, rot, and moss growth.

SIMPLE DESIGN

A fully outfitted gazebo would be too much of a distraction from the pretty scene and ocean view, so the homeowners kept it simple, and you can, too. It's as easy as ordering a gazebo kit online and assembling it yourself—no contractor required! One source with lots of options and detailed instructions is Amish Country Gazebos; amishgazebos.com.

LUSH LANDSCAPING

Thanks to vine-covered walls and posts that bring the flora inside the gazebo, this simple shelter blends seamlessly in the midst of a wild garden.

PULL IT TOGETHER

PUT DOWN…
a durable surface

No matter if your outdoor living room is as simple as a pergola-covered deck or as finished as a freestanding pavilion, you still need a surface that will stand up to moisture and heat. Brick and tile floors are smart options for covered spaces because they're long-lasting, low-maintenance, and won't get slick under a roof. Both flooring types offer opportunities for customization: Bricks can be laid in a pattern, like herringbone, while tile can add color to the space. An outdoor rug that can be hosed down when needed will soften the surface and make the room more inviting.

FURNISH WITH…
all-weather seating

The best way to design a furniture plan for your pavilion, pergola, or gazebo is to approach it the same way you would an indoor living room, which typically features a mix of seating types (sofas, love seats, club chairs). After taking into account how you plan to use the space and what aesthetic you prefer, pick pieces that can be left outside all year long. Teak seating constructed with mortise-and-tenon joinery (two pieces of wood joined at a 90-degree angle with interlocking posts and holes) is a timeless option that's naturally water resistant. Woven seating made of weatherproof resin is a durable alternative to iconic wicker and rattan pieces. Metal furniture comes in a variety of colors and styles but must be kept sealed to prevent rust. Comfort is key for lingering outside, so be sure to look for pieces with plush cushions upholstered in soft, water- and fade-resistant fabrics.

TOP IT OFF WITH…
lighting

Welcoming rooms are illuminated by multiple sources, from ceiling lights to wall fixtures. Outdoor hanging pendants, flush-mount fixtures, and sconces come in all kinds of shapes and power sources (candle, gas, or electric). Choose metal fixtures with finishes that will not corrode or rust, like oil-rubbed bronze or stainless steel. To add softer light, incorporate floor or table lamps, either suitable for outdoor use (with resin bases and water-resistant shades) or lightweight indoor versions that are easy to stow away when bad weather arises.

CONSIDER ADDING…
window treatments

Just as most indoor living rooms look bare without window treatments, pavilions, pergolas, and gazebos feel more finished with curtains, shades, or blinds, too; in fact, their light- and temperature-regulating functions are even more important outside. Sheer drapes and woven blinds filter harsh sunlight without blocking views. Heavier lined curtains made of weatherproof fabric add privacy as well as warmth by blocking wind and trapping heat during cooler months. Louvered shutters control the intensity of breezes, while traditional planked versions can shut out wind altogether.

4

KITCHENS, DINING AREAS & BARS

Hosting friends and family for an alfresco dinner can be as simple as grilling, eating at a picnic table, and serving beer from a cooler—or it can involve preparing a full meal at a built-in outdoor kitchen, dining on comfortable furniture, and mixing drinks at a fully stocked bar. Both accomplish one of life's great pleasures: sharing a meal with friends or family. These outdoor kitchen, dining, and bar ideas will inspire you to transform your outdoor space into party central.

rock solid

Built into stacked-stone walls and tucked under a cedar ceiling, this full-service outdoor kitchen and dining area is protected from the elements and designed for all-season use.

SHELTERED SPACE

By pushing the outdoor kitchen and dining room into a recessed nook under the house, these home-owners are able to entertain outside in all types of weather. Stone walls and a cedar ceiling are great insulators, which means this kitchen is cool during the summer and warm during the winter. The heavy-duty materials also protect the appliances and furniture when the space is not being used.

LACQUERED TRAYS

Not only are they indestructible, but lacquered trays like the one by this grill are also useful for corralling table linens, setting up a self-serve beverage bar, and carrying items back and forth between a main kitchen and an outdoor one.

BAR-HEIGHT TABLE

With its industrial metal base, the tall table is the perfect place to gather for drinks on cushy barstools while someone supervises the grill.

Material Matters

The built-in grill, range, refrigerator, and cabinets (which conceal fuel tanks) are stainless steel, thus impenetrable to water damage. Routine polishing helps ensure they look their best.

poolside perch

Positioned on the patio of an infinity-edge pool that overlooks the ocean, this table and chairs gives new meaning to waterfront dining.

PAINTED FURNITURE

Rendered in a semigloss white finish, these traditional dining chairs and table take on a more casual look. Bring indoors during inclement weather, or choose all-weather options like teak or powder-coated metal.

PRINTED CUSHIONS

Patterned fabric in sunny yellow and crisp white softens these seats and infuses the whole dining setup with cheerful whimsy. Extra-long fabric ties lend flirty, feminine style.

ACRYLIC GLASSWARE

Made of synthetic polymers (a form of plastic), these wineglasses are nearly indestructible, making them a good poolside pick.

inside out

Built-in appliances (including a dishwasher!), plenty of storage, and a super comfy seating area centered around a fireplace make this outdoor kitchen as well equipped as any indoor version.

COUNTER SPACE

Concrete countertops wrap around the entire perimeter, providing plenty of prep and serving space. If you don't have this much room, 6-foot-long counters are large enough to fit most built-in grills and still leave room on either side to store tableware and prepare side dishes.

CUSTOM CABINETRY

Forget making trips back inside for another plate or glass. Thanks to a hutch-style cabinet and drawer space, these homeowners can store cooking tools and serving pieces outside. The cabinet drawer and door faces are wood, which requires sealing inside and out every few years (unlike the sturdy painted brick).

OPEN SEATING

People congregate in kitchens, whether inside or out. In keeping with indoor floor plan trends, this cook space is open to the seating area—complete with loveseats and armchairs, a soft rug, and a cozy fireplace—which functions like an outdoor family room. The whole space is covered by a latticed roof, which creates a little shade but does not completely close in the room.

--- ***Material Matters*** ---

Concrete countertops are great for outdoor kitchens because they blend in with other hardscape surfaces like stone, can be tinted any shade, and are extremely durable. Most cement mixes will, however, develop cracks over time and thus must be sealed once a year to prevent water damage.

Steal This Idea

If your grill is under a pergola or other roof structure, consider installing a ceiling fan to help carry away smoke and circulate fresh air.

Steal This Idea

For a simpler outdoor dining setup, skip the built-in bar and roll out a bar cart loaded with your favorite spirits and mixers instead.

open air

This outdoor kitchen proves all it takes for a great alfresco dinner party is pizza, a crowd-accommodating table, and a few cold beverages.

SIMPLE DESIGN
Because this space is just off the indoor kitchen, the homeowners skipped adding a sink and refrigerator. Instead, they focused on incorporating elements their main kitchen lacked, like a stand-alone grill.

PIZZA OVEN
Wood-fired pizza ovens are often sold as inserts, so these homeowners designed and built a smooth concrete supporting structure that complements the other cement and stone hardscape surfaces in their yard. Like charcoal grills, pizza ovens take up to 30 minutes to get hot, but once the fire is ready, it will cook a pizza to crunchy delight in just a few minutes.

EXTRA-LONG TABLE
The streamlined wood-and-stainless steel table is perfect for a party. It seats a crowd of up to 12 for dinner and also makes a spacious hors d'oeuvres serving station for a cocktail party.

fully stocked

With its ocean-inspired backsplash and pretty white countertop and shelves, this backyard bar creates a true vacation vibe at home.

SMART STORAGE

Open shelving, ample counter space, and lower cabinets are the perfect combo for a hardworking bar. The floating ledges display what's available and keep glasses at the ready, making it easy for guests to serve themselves; the cabinets below store larger platters, serving trays, and linens.

TILED BACKSPLASH

Shimmering penny-round tiles in various shades of blue transform the bar's back wall into a colorful statement. Beyond their good looks, the tiles are practically damage-resistant and are simple to clean when splashes and spills occur.

PEDESTAL ICE BUCKET

Keep cool drinks within reach when you use an ice bucket on a pedestal: an elegant alternative to a cooler parked on the ground for serving frosty libations. Another idea: Fill a drink dispenser with a signature cocktail for quick refills.

Steal This Idea
Pipe the sounds of your stereo outside with speakers. Mount them on an exterior wall, or bring portable, wireless speakers outside when entertaining.

natural romance

Lush foliage, organic textures, ample seating, and elegant table settings add up to a dreamy dining area.

CRAWLING VINES

The thick, hearty vines wrapped around this pergola provide shade and protection from wind, making long meals more comfortable. Fast-growing vines like wisteria will cover an entire supporting structure in as little as one season, but they also require routine trimming to ensure they do not damage the exterior of your house.

TRESTLE TABLE

Thanks to its base, which features two sets of legs connected by a cross-member that runs lengthwise, this teak table is extremely sturdy and stable—an important consideration when choosing outdoor tables because they're often placed on uneven surfaces, like this brick patio, and are exposed to the elements.

PLUSH SEATS

These soft chair cushions are upholstered in weatherproof fabric, making them impervious to sun or water damage. Adding fabric ties keeps the cushions in place in case of strong breezes.

fine dining

Furnished with soft drapes, sophisticated pendant lights, and traditional dining chairs, this alfresco setup has all the panache of a formal indoor dining room.

OUTDOOR CURTAINS

These curtains soften the hardscape and provide a buffer from strong winds; their green fabric tape trim complements the palette of the house's architecture and natural surroundings, as well as the pool furniture.

LANTERN LIGHTING

A symmetrical pair of brass pendants, reminiscent of indoor lighting, gives this outdoor dining room an elegant air. Because the table is nestled under a curtain-lined loggia, the lanterns are protected from gusty winds.

TRADITIONAL SEATING

Although dressed down in teak, this combination of host and hostess armchairs and armless dining chairs echoes seating styles found in more formal indoor settings.

Steal This Idea

For a more casual take on table settings, switch out linen napkins for striped kitchen towels. The soft, absorbent fabric is perfect for protecting laps, cleaning sticky fingers, and wiping up spills.

au naturel

Weathered wood surfaces, a stone patio, and accessories in shades of khaki, gray, and green keep the focus of this uncovered dining area on its natural surroundings.

BANQUETTE SEATING
Decked out with weatherproof pillows, this wrap-around banquette can accommodate a crowd. It's also built into a foliage-lined partial concrete wall, which provides privacy, some protection from the elements, and a noise buffer from neighbors.

DECORATIVE ACCENTS
Even simple setups look more finished with a few flourishes, such as this hanging wooden mirror. When choosing accessories, think about what you might select if the space were inside—then look for options made of weatherproof materials.

FOLDING CHAIRS
These canvas, teak, and chrome director's-style chairs are comfortable and durable. Furthermore, their foldable design and lightweight construction make them easy to reconfigure for parties of different sizes, or to store inside when not needed.

PULL IT TOGETHER

FIRE IT UP WITH…
a grill
Outdoor dining isn't the same without cooking over an open flame—and there's so much more to grilling than just cooking meat. Serious outdoor cooks will need ample counter space for prep, and thus should opt for a built-in grill with a flange. If you plan to cook and eat outside only occasionally, a stand-alone grill will do the trick. Consider models with fold-down side extensions for extra prep and storage space. Gas-fueled grills heat up faster and are easier to clean, but some grill masters swear charcoal-fueled options contribute more flavor.

CONSIDER ADDING A…
built-in counter
Not only does a counter give an outdoor kitchen a more finished look and make prepping for meals much easier, but it also doubles as a serving spot once everything is cooked. Outdoor counters are typically built with bricks, stucco, ceramic tile, wood cabinets, or stone that complements the style of the house, patio, and garden. When it comes to countertops, durability should be the top priority. Softer stones like limestone and marble are not ideal for outdoor use, but other common indoor countertop materials, like granite, concrete, ceramic tile, or composite quartz, hold up well. Brick and flagstone are also great long-lasting options.

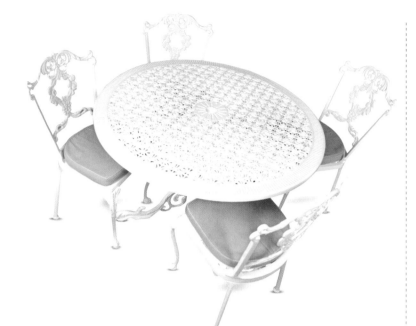

ADD AMBIENCE WITH…
festive lighting
In nearly every other outdoor space, lighting is more functional than mood enhancing. But when it comes to illuminating entertaining areas, think festive—without, of course, ignoring usefulness. For a classic outdoor café vibe, string up twinkly lights with translucent globes (sometimes called café lights) under a pergola or around an umbrella. Colorful paper lanterns serve the same purpose but have a more bohemian style. You can never go wrong with candlelight outside, from glass lanterns atop tables for a warm glow to votive cups or torches lining pathways or patio perimeters. Just be sure to keep open flames away from plants to avoid a fire.

FURNISH IT WITH…
a table and chairs
The most important consideration when shopping for outdoor dining furniture is finding the right balance between stability and flexibility. Tables should be sturdy enough to maintain their balance during wind gusts, while chairs need to be lightweight enough to move easily. Outdoor tables and chairs are available in a wide variety of weather-resistant materials, from teak to powder-coated metal. Rectangular tables typically seat more people and provide plenty of space for serving platters, but round tables are more likely to come with a hole in the center for an umbrella. One other consideration: Although slatted tabletops are more common, solid versions protect laps from spilled drinks.

5
POOLS &
CABANAS

One way to bring the spirit of vacation to your home is by installing a pool. The look, feel, and sound of water have restorative effects similar to those of spending time at the beach or lake. Pools also transform a typical outdoor space into an oasis designed for play, relaxation, and even a little exercise. Keep in mind how you plan to use your pool when deciding on its shape, size, and design: Small, shallow plunge pools (no deeper than 4 feet) are all you need for refreshing dips; long, skinny (and still shallow) pools are geared toward swimming laps; and larger pools work well for general use. These pool and cabana design ideas will have you booking staycations in your backyard.

courtyard paradise

Tucked behind a privacy wall and between two wings of a U-shaped house, this plunge pool has the feel of an upscale hotel.

PARTIALLY SUBMERGED CHAISES
A pair of chaise longues that sits in 6-inch-deep water provides the perfect pad for sunbathing. Although the teak frames are naturally resistant to rot, the chairs should not be left in the water for more than a few days at a time.

SWIM-UP CABANA
Being able to swim to shelter—or step right from the shaded cabana into the water—not only maximizes the courtyard's limited space but also adds a luxurious, exotic feel. Trimmed curtains capped by a Greek fret-style valance complete the resort-inspired look.

LOUNGE SEATING
Simple lines, generous proportions, plush cushions, and a black-painted resin finish make these sofas and chairs just as comfortable as they are sophisticated.

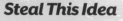

Steal This Idea
Consider installing a pool-side fountain to hear the tranquil sound of running water. Jets in the wall create simple fountains with just enough splash to provide soothing background noise.

Steal This Idea

Made of water-resistant sailcloth, this extra-durable fence has a modern edge, protects the low-slung chaises from strong wind, and provides a little privacy for sunbathers without completely blocking the ocean view.

modern gem

From the minimalist furnishings to the water level that's flush with the deck's edge, this saltwater pool's ultrastreamlined design shows just how soothing simplicity can be.

EDGELESS PERIMETER
This pool has the same sleek look, integrated feel, and engineering of an infinity pool. To facilitate the disappearing edge, a narrow trough, or basin, runs around the perimeter of the pool to catch and recycle spillover water.

HIGH-TECH CHAISES
Powered by hydraulic lifts beneath the pool deck, these frameless chaises, which appear to float next to the water, can be raised and lowered at the touch of a button.

SHADED SOFA
At the far end of the pool, a simple structure offers some shade over the sofa without taking up much space on the pool deck.

Material Matters

Although saltwater pools do not have the byproducts associated with traditional chlorine-producing systems, they are not entirely chemical-free. The salt in these pools produces a continuous supply of chlorine through a process called electrolysis. Saltwater pools depend on chlorine levels, tracked by an underwater monitor, to remain clean.

woodland sanctuary

The rocks, abundant plantings, and soaring trees that surround this pool make it feel more like a natural spring than a created one.

ATYPICAL SHAPE
For swimmers, this pool's long, narrow profile re-creates the sensation of following a creek as it flows through the woods.

ROCK LINING
Large rocks that jut out over the surface of the water give the pool's sides a more organic, rather than straight, edge. The rocks also help swimmers feel more connected to their surroundings.

LUSH LANDSCAPING
Tucked into the back of this lot, the pool is bordered on two sides by landscaping, which shades the pool during certain times of day.

tropical lagoon

Framed by a disappearing edge and lined with tiles that make the water appear the same color as the ocean, this pool and cabana feel like extensions of the rocky coast and expansive blue sea beyond.

INFINITY EDGE

From the perspective of a swimmer submerged in the water, there's almost no distinguishing where this pool ends and the ocean begins besides a small rocky landscape in between. Just because you don't have an ocean view doesn't mean you should rule out an edgeless pool, though. Consider them for hillsides to create the illusion of water running into the sky's horizon line, or for a modern twist on traditional deck-lined pools.

DARK BOTTOM

Tiles lining this pool basin create the illusion of dark blue water, which has a more natural feel. Dark-bottomed pools also create a mirrored effect on the surface, reflecting the surrounding landscape and absorbing more heat from the sun for warmer water.

MINIMALIST LIGHTS

After the sun goes down, can lights mounted on cabana posts cast a warm glow on both the surface of the water and the structure itself without detracting from the cabana's simplicity during the day.

palm spring

Capped on either end by open-air pavilions, lined by an allée of royal palms, and surrounded by soft green grass, this lap pool has a timeless, formal look.

SYMMETRICAL DESIGN

This classic backyard is a study in symmetry: The same scene, featuring two gazebos boasting louvered-paneled entrances flanked by matching potted palms, repeats on either end of the long, narrow pool.

IRIDESCENT TILES

A border of mosaic tiles gives the illusion of a waterfall edge and creates a subdued, sophisticated look; for a lively twist, try a multicolor tile border.

ADJOINING SPA

It doesn't get more relaxing than soaking in a spa or hot tub after a long day. In-ground spas like this one share a water filtration and heating system with the connected pool. A low hedge of shrubs along the sides and palms planted near the corners give the spa the same classic style as the pool.

island oasis

With its wide deck, generous proportions, shaded corner, and panoramic views, this pool makes the most of its island hilltop location.

SHELTERED SLEEP SPOT
Furnished with a bed made up with outdoor fabrics, this pavilion-style cabana provides a cool respite from the sun for an afternoon siesta. Louvered Bermuda shutters along two sides of the structure allow shade seekers to control the breezes.

DUAL STEPS
Instead of one wide set of steps running the entire width of the pool, two slender sets run down each side of the pool, a minimalist look that leaves more space for swimming and floating. The two staircases are joined by a shallow ledge—the ideal spot for partially submerged sunbathing.

GIANT POTTED PALMS
The homeowners didn't want to plant large trees or shrubs that might grow to obstruct the pretty views, but they still yearned for plenty of greenery to tie into the soft, lush landscape of the sloping hill leading to the water. The solution: extra-large cement planters with leafy green palms lined up along the perimeter of the expansive wood deck.

backyard beauty

Located just behind the house's back patio, this pool's ample size is perfect for parties, while its symmetrical design and pretty details give it timeless appeal.

CLASSIC SHAPE
The rectangular pool not only suits the layout of the lot and house but also provides maximum function: It's long enough for laps and wide enough to accommodate a crowd. Rounded corners finish off the superfunctional swimming spot with a little extra polish.

BUILT-IN SEATING
A pair of concrete benches attached to the patio creates a lounge spot on the part of the pool deck that's not deep enough for chaises. Cushions and umbrellas add comfort.

COLORFUL BEDS
Planted with orange bromeliads, these four beds add bright color to the pool's perimeter without requiring extra maintenance. This perennial, a relative of the pineapple plant, does not need much water, colors up best in full sun, and has no serious pests.

PULL IT TOGETHER

CHOOSE…
a pool basin surface

There's more to pool design than shape and depth. The basin surface determines the color of the water. The most basic surface is white plaster, which gives water a clean, bright blue appearance. White plaster is the most economical surface, but it's also more susceptible to chemical damage than newer products. Basic plaster can also be tinted to shift the appearance of the water's color. For a wider range of hues and increased resistance to the effects of chemicals, consider a surface made of plaster mixed with colored ceramic quartz. The newest product on the market, pebble surfaces also come in a range of colors and are the most impervious to chemical damage. These natural surfaces, however, are more expensive and rougher to the touch than plaster.

CHOOSE…
smooth decking

When it comes to selecting a pool deck surface, texture is the most important consideration, at least for the sake of all those bare feet that will walk on it. The best surfaces are smooth—but not so slick that they cause swimmers to slip when getting out of the pool. Light-colored surfaces retain less heat from the sun and are thus less likely to burn feet. Material options include: brick, which has a traditional, timeless look but must be monitored for moss growth; natural wood and lower-maintenance composite wood; and concrete pavers, which should be scored or brushed to prevent them from becoming slippery when wet.

PULL UP…
comfy chaise longues

Aside from weather resistance, the most important aspect of selecting a chaise longue is comfort. Look for chaises that are adjustable and provide support where you need it. As with other outdoor furniture, the most durable materials are teak, which can be topped with soft cushions in any color or pattern; metal, which often incorporates built-in woven fabric seating (thus not requiring cushions) that can be hosed down; or woven resin, which resembles traditional wicker or rattan but will not rot when exposed to rain.

COOL DOWN UNDER…
a cabana

Designed to provide a respite from the sun, these structures can be as primitive or as elaborate as you'd like. If all you're looking for is a shady spot to sit for a bit, a simple post-and-beam structure with enough space for a chair or two is all you need. The wall-less design will prevent shade-seekers from feeling closed in. For additional protection from the sun and wind, consider draping your cabana with outdoor curtains or lining it with louvered shutters.

6
OUTDOOR SHOWERS

Nothing embraces the carefree spirit of beach life like an outdoor shower. Adding one is simpler than you'd think: All it takes is a water source, somewhere for the water to drain, and a privacy screen. (An ocean view is not required!) This chapter offers suggestions on how to design a shower with almost any look or feel. So kick off your flip-flops and hop on in—you'll feel like you're running through a backyard sprinkler without a care in the world.

traditional charm

White-painted clapboard siding, a blue hydrangea-lined pea gravel path, and a vintage life preserver are a no-fail combination for a time-honored, coastal look.

LOCATION, LOCATION, LOCATION

Building an outdoor shower that taps into an existing water source will cause the fewest hassles for your contractor—and put the least strain on your budget. For access to hot and cold water, look for space along an exterior wall on the other side of an interior bath or kitchen.

LOW-MAINTENANCE MATERIALS

Once painted or treated with another sealant, standard decking (like this raised wooden platform) and exterior siding (like these painted clapboards) can handle moisture without any additional upkeep. Narrow gaps between the deck boards allow water to pass through.

NAUTICAL NOD

Small gestures, like a blue-and-white striped towel and classic life preserver, add seafaring style to this otherwise simple, utilitarian shower.

Material Matters

Pea gravel is a good option for a path leading to an outdoor shower because it allows water to filter down to absorbent dirt and prevents landscape erosion by serving as a ground cover.

minimalist spa

Streamlined fixtures, the absence of a privacy screen or fence, and a manmade flooring surface are a fresh take on the outdoor shower.

OPEN-AIR DESIGN
Not every outdoor shower needs an enclosure, especially if its primary purpose is for rinsing off sand before, or chlorine after, a dip in the pool. This one is mounted along the same wall as the plunge pool fountain, which simplified plumbing.

LUXE FIXTURE
A rain-style showerhead plus a handheld attachment bring the comforts of a spa shower outside.

SLIP-RESISTANT FLOORING
The homeowners replaced slick white tiles with Astroturf for more sure-footed showers. The evergreen artificial grass allows water from the shower to empty into an underground drainage system.

tropical hideaway

Bamboo fencing, tree trunk posts, and a few potted plants give this DIY outdoor shower an island paradise feel.

SIMPLE CONSTRUCTION
This rustic shower is built with ready-made materials—bamboo fencing, locust tree trunk posts (which are very strong and tend to be straighter than other tree trunks), and a showerhead affixed to an existing outdoor spigot.

NO-SLIP DRAINAGE
Permeable round concrete pavers provide a slick-free place to stand, while loose gravel filters water into the ground. Bonus: The combo creates a fun pattern underfoot.

HARDY VEGETATION
Banana trees, ornamental grasses, and a smattering of smaller potted plants make this outdoor shower reminiscent of a tropical jungle.

double duty

Whimsical, brightly colored animal sculptures give these side-by-side rinsing stations a cheerful, happy-go-lucky vibe.

LOCKER ROOM SETUP
For large families or those who have lots of guests, this design will cut down on wait times for the outdoor showers. The board-and-batten construction and lockable doors, which offer plenty of privacy, are like camp baths.

WATER-RESISTANT ARTWORK
These wall hangings add a colorful jolt of life to the white showers—and they won't deteriorate in the face of day-in, day-out exposure to moisture, thanks to their glazed finish.

HOOK HANG-UPS
Large hooks (painted white) in between the showers and on the backs of the doors keep towels on hand and prevent swimming gear from getting lost.

simply modern

With its horizontal slatted-screen construction, striped outdoor rug, and clipped boxwood, this outdoor shower shows off just how smart simple can look.

DRESSING ROOM ADDITION

If you have space, consider carving out a nook for stripping down and covering up. Outfitted with a bench and wall of hooks, this changing room makes it easy to get dressed after rinsing off.

PLENTY OF PRIVACY

Composed of horizontal cedar boards, this slatted screen shields bathers from view without making the space feel too closed in.

ALL-WEATHER RUG

A striped indoor/outdoor rug not only adds a pop of color to the all-wood area but also doubles as a bath mat for drying wet feet.

Material Matters

Thanks to naturally occurring rot-resistant compounds, wood species like cedar are a clever pick for outdoor shower construction.

PULL IT TOGETHER

CHOOSE…
an exterior wall

Installing a shower fixture on the side of the house allows you to tap into existing plumbing lines. If your exterior siding is in good condition, it can handle the extra splashes from the shower. Siding materials that are particularly resistant to moisture include cedar-shake shingles, fiber cement siding, or freshly painted wood.

PUT DOWN…
a well-draining floor

Before building an outdoor shower, consider how you'll use it. If you plan to use soap and shampoo, opt for concrete slab floors and ensure that the drainage is connected to your sewer or septic system to prevent runoff from harming nearby plants. For simple rinses, almost any flooring type, from raised wooden decks (which allow water to drain through) to pavers and gravel, will do, so long as it prevents water from pooling next to your house. As a safety precaution, be sure you choose floor material that's not slippery.

INSTALL…
a showerhead

For wall-mounted showers, look for fixtures with finishes that will stand up to the elements outside, such as rust-resistant stainless steel or oil-rubbed bronze that's not likely to corrode. Freestanding showers that can be hooked up to exterior spigots offer a flexible alternative to fixed-mount fixtures, but they typically provide only cold water.

CLOSE IT OFF WITH…
a privacy screen

The type of enclosure you'll want depends on how you plan to use your outdoor shower. For quick rinses, partial walls or screens made with open-air designs like louvers or lattice will suffice. For full-body cleanings, consider hanging a removable shower curtain (that can be stored when not in use) or building full-height walls from a moisture-tolerant wood like cedar, cypress, or black locust.

7
PATIOS, DECKS & DOCKS

Patios, decks, and docks offer total exposure to all that nature has to offer. Patios are the most versatile and easiest to construct; they can be adjacent to your house as an extension of indoor space or stand-alone features that serve as destination spots. Docks can be more than just places to secure a boat when designed like a deck on stilts. Here's how to get a comfortable spot for soaking up the sun.

classic charm

Against a backdrop of gray shingles, white trim, and blue shutters, this brick-trimmed patio decked with blue and white textiles exemplifies timeless seaside decor.

BLUESTONE AND BRICK
The blue-gray shade of the stone echoes the palette of the house, while the geometric pattern of the brick trim adds visual interest. When installing a patio adjacent to your house, make sure your contractor grades the surface away from the home to prevent water damage.

DOUBLE-DUTY LOUNGING
Because they had plenty of space, the homeowners created two seating areas with distinct functions: chaises for sunbathing, and armchairs and an ottoman for reading or talking. Dividing a large patio into separate areas makes each feel more intimate and welcoming.

OVERSIZE LANTERNS
When it comes to candlelight, size matters: the bigger the better for casting a warm, inviting glow. Shapely lanterns add charm even when the candles aren't lit.

organic refuge

Raised plant beds and plant-lined pavers surround this well-appointed patio with verdant softness, easing the transition between it and the garden beyond.

PLANT-LINED PAVERS
Installing concrete pavers directly on top of existing grass creates a natural geometric pattern and a balance between hard and soft surfaces. Bonus: The combination of exposed ground plus permeable pavers minimizes water runoff.

RAISED BED
This concrete planter creates a lush green perimeter around the patio and doubles as extra seating.

COMFY OTTOMANS
Cube-shaped poufs upholstered in outdoor fabric are a smart solution for flexible patio furnishings. On their own, they're extra-cushy seats; pulled up to a chair, sofa, or love seat, they provide a place for propping up feet.

modern comfort

Sleek surfaces juxtaposed with a cozy fireplace and teak seating give this patio a clean and contemporary, but not at all austere, feel.

STREAMLINED FIREPLACE
A pair of unadorned openings (one for the firebox and one for wood storage), concealed chimney, and stark white, mantel-less design bring a clean aesthetic and simple warmth to this fireplace. When constructing outdoor fireplaces (or placing other heat sources), position them away from tree branches or potted plants for safety.

STONE FLOOR
Irregularly shaped, colored, and textured stone provides a natural contrast to the super smooth and squared-off fireplace. Locally quarried stone is typically less expensive and more eco-friendly; it also gives your patio a native, aged look.

NICKEL LANTERNS
Metal fixtures add a touch of mod shine to the patio. Nickel-plated fixtures and hardware are durable and well-suited to outdoor use.

Steal This Idea

Floor cushions create super flexible seating on a deck or patio. Stack a few to fashion a chair, or spread them out for lounging.

camp ground

Butterfly chairs, a hammock, and a few tarps strung up on posts for shade make this deck feel like a serene sanctuary in the midst of the wilderness.

CANVAS SEATING
Butterfly chairs and a hammock conform to the sitter's body shape for a surprisingly comfortable seat. Both are also wise picks for exposed decks because they're made of weather-resistant materials.

SHADE TARPS
A few posts or tree trunks, tarps, and rope are all it takes to shield your deck from the sun. One advantage to a temporary shade source like this one is that the setup can be reconfigured as the sun moves throughout the day.

WILD MEADOW
The unmanicured grassy space that separates this deck from the main house makes the raised wooden platform overlooking the ocean feel like a rustic refuge in the backcountry. More important, the native grasses are also extremely low-maintenance.

rooftop retreat

The dining and seating areas, potted privacy screen, and colorful cabinetry with a mini-fridge and fully stocked bar make this roof deck suitable for sunbathing, dining, or stargazing.

PAINTED FLOOR
The smooth gray-painted cement surface of this roof deck is a low-maintenance alternative to more traditional types of decking. Look for paint formulated for porch, patio, and floor application, and consider topping it off with an anti-slip coating.

COLORFUL STORAGE
Bright green built-in cabinets line the perimeter of the roof deck and hold towels, games, and drink supplies for easy entertaining. For weather-resistant options, try cabinets made of a synthetic material or woods like teak or cypress.

PRIVACY HEDGE
Drought-resistant plants such as New Zealand flax and succulents potted in raised beds and shallow pots atop the cabinetry screen the deck from neighbors.

green peace

With its green tree canopy, feathery potted plants, and panoramic view, this unadorned deck is blissfully exposed to the elements.

UNINTERRUPTED VIEW
The lack of railings on this deck means nothing gets between you, your chaise longue, and that seemingly endless water vista. The open design also facilitates easy water access and is best suited for shallow shorelines like this one.

POTTED PLANTS
Marking off the corners and sides of this dock with leafy plants in oversize, colorful pots adds natural texture and serves as a boundary for its edge. Bonus: Hearing the leaves rustle in the breeze will complement the seaside soundtrack.

NATURAL SHADE
There may be no need for an umbrella when your dock is shaded by the leafy branches of a nearby tree like this one.

sun seeker

With its upholstered banquettes and rattan ottomans, this deck is a super comfortable spot for kicking back and soaking up the sun.

BANQUETTE SEATING

Built-in love seats made from the same timbers that were used to construct the deck's railing are a simple, wallet-friendly alternative to furnishing a deck with stand-alone seating. Red-striped cushions add cheer, while the wide railing serves as extra seating during cocktail hour.

TOWEL STORAGE

A tall woven basket with a lid keeps fresh towels dry and handy. Another idea: Include a storage nook beneath the seat of built-in benches or banquettes to make space for towels and life preservers.

PALM BORDER

A row of low palms planted along the perimeter of the deck conceals its raised foundation and the empty space underneath. If you don't live in a coastal area, clipped boxwoods, lavender, or native grasses work just as well.

PULL IT TOGETHER

CHOOSE…
a long-lasting hardscape

Concrete, brick, and treated or composite wood are the best bets for a lounge surface that will withstand the tests of time, weather, and heavy use. When choosing a patio material, be sure to consider those used on the exterior of the house for a more seamless look. Permeable concrete, brick, and stone pavers are all hardy, nonslippery options with distinct looks. Try mixing materials or adding a border for extra panache. For decks and docks, use either pressure-treated or composite wood (made of sawdust and recycled plastic) for durability. Composite lumber won't splinter and is resistant to rot, whereas wood decking comes with a more natural aesthetic—and seasonal maintenance like sanding and sealing.

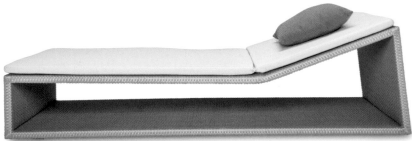

FURNISH WITH…
lounge seating

From deep armchairs with ottomans to sleek, minimalist chaise longues, outdoor seating designed for reclining comes in a variety of styles and materials. As with other outdoor spaces, choose patio and deck chairs based on how you plan to use them: Chaise longues are best for napping *en plein air* while armchairs and ottomans are better suited for facilitating conversation while soaking up the sun. A luxuriously cozy alternative to lounge chairs and chaises is outdoor daybeds, but keep in mind that mattresses will need to be stored when not in use.

FINISH IT OFF WITH…
potted plants

As the ultimate transition spaces between your home and your yard, patios, decks, and even docks look best when decorated with a little green. Potted plants not only soften the hardscape of patio and deck surfaces, but also help define boundaries, add privacy, and modulate noise. Terra-cotta, glazed ceramic, and stone planters are heavy-duty options, while resin versions are a lightweight but still weather-resistant alternative. Other ways to incorporate lush greenery include installing a vine-covered trellis or planting a low hedge around the perimeter of your deck or patio.

CONSIDER ADDING…
a shade source

For a respite from UV rays that still allows you to enjoy the fresh air and take in the views, incorporate an element that offers partial shade on your patio, deck, or dock. Umbrellas that can be adjusted or simple canvas tarps that can be strung up between fence posts offer flexibility.

gardening

There's no activity better than growing a garden to connect you with nature. For outdoor enthusiasts, the satisfaction of working with your hands in the dirt, and then enjoying the fruits of your labor, is almost unsurpassed. But if you weren't born with a green thumb, fear not: Creating outdoor "rooms" that stimulate the senses is easier than it may appear—even along the coast, where harsh conditions like salty air and wind prevail. The gardens on the following pages are packed with ideas for how to foster one that thrives in the face of nearly any challenge, from pests to persnickety weather.

8
CLASSIC GARDENS

Picture a traditional garden and some key elements come to mind: stacked stone, riotous blooms, peaceful paths, stately seating, formal courtyards, natural prairies. They're places that must be both hardworking and beautiful. Here, we've gathered our favorite examples, from California to Maine.

opposites attract

This combination of green foliage, secluded sitting areas, and fragrant borders creates an English manor garden feel in Mendocino, California.

CALM RETREAT
This formal sunken garden—complete with a lily pond and water channel that divides a manicured lawn—provides a quiet, protected place to read and reflect just outside the master bedroom.

DOUBLE DUTY & RECYCLED BEAUTY
Rammed-earth walls (formed with dirt from the site, mixed with sand and cement, and capped with concrete slabs) that surround the courtyard spared the owner from having to truck away excavated soil. Lining the retaining walls with verdant ground covers re-creates the feel of an English garden.

MIGHTY MIX
This 3-acre plot manages to combine formed spaces like courtyards clustered near the house with looser natural prairies as the landscape opens up to the ocean.

GUARDED BEAUTY
Natural wind blockers like a thick hedge of Victorian box behind a bench or the screen of purple leaf plum trees lining the sunken courtyard work with the topography to protect the property from strong coastal winds.

GREEN WAYS
Mowed grass paths that meander through densely planted flower beds are a soft and colorful alternative to typical stone paths, especially in a garden filled with green foliage.

SHAPE SHIFTER
Throughout this garden, a series of five arched gates made of black acacia wood are modeled after the house's Craftsman-style windows and painted the same green for a simple but effective architectural tie-in.

Steal This Idea
Use reclaimed bricks to create bed borders. Lay them at an angle or flat, or mix it up in different areas of the yard.

storybook charm

At this seaside getaway in Delaware, small outdoor "rooms" with manicured hedges, stacked-stone walls, and plenty of seating create cozy retreats.

WELL-MADE PLANS
When designing the various outdoor rooms, these home-owners picked out and installed the garden's hardscape and furnishings—benches, sculpture, an arbor, pathways, a fish pond and fountain, a gravel courtyard—long before thinking about what kinds of plants would highlight them.

PRETTY, FUNCTIONAL SPACES
Even the raised vegetable bed just outside the kitchen door exudes a cottage garden aesthetic, thanks to a Chippendale gate, a pair of pink phlox-filled urns, and lavender-lined tuteurs that support tomato plants.

LOW MAINTENANCE
Defined mostly by shrubs and trees like hydrangea, Japanese holly, ivy, 'Carefree Delight' roses, and dwarf weeping cherry trees, this garden requires little year-round upkeep, which gives the owners more time to enjoy it.

COLOR TIES

When it came time to plant the garden, the owners chose a palette of green, white, and violet with pops of pink that echo the shades of the house and hardscapes. For example, sculpted boxwoods, lush lawns, and ivy-covered walls pick up the forest green shutters and doors, while blue nepeta, 'Nikko Blue' hydrangea, lilacs, and lavender tie in with the crushed blue slate gravel paths and slate paver patio.

GRASSLESS COURTYARDS

Instead of a traditional front lawn, the homeowners created two shrub-enclosed courtyards that center on dwarf weeping cherry trees and are filled with blue nepeta. Liriope lines the brick walkway.

COOL COVER-UP

Fast-growing ivy camouflages a plain garage wall with soothing green foliage, creating a more natural-looking boundary for the vegetable garden. Cutting the vine back three times a season keeps its growth in check.

raised expectations

Ingenuity plus savvy plant picks protect this coastal Maine garden from flooding and a thriving deer population.

PAVED WAY
This gorgeous 1,800-square-foot plot was once a mere parking pad. Now, gravel walkways between raised beds reduce rainwater runoff and suppress weeds.

NATURAL COURSE
Beyond the gravel courtyard, the homeowners stuck to native trees and shrubs, such as paper birch and spruce, to increase the garden's survival odds and visually link it to the natural landscape.

CREATURE COMFORTS
This lawn-less garden is serene, with plenty of makeshift places to sit and take in the garden's sights and fragrances. Even the walls of raised beds serve as seating during outdoor parties.

ELEVATED GOODS
Stacked fieldstone frames the 2-foot-high raised beds, which allow for better drainage for the lady's-mantle, Russian sage, chives, and anise hyssop on this flood-prone site.

FRAGRANT PROTECTION
Onion-scented alliums, as well as other plants with pungent aromas, repel hungry deer. Perennials with gray or felted foliage have a similar effect, but without the odor.

SUPPORT SYSTEM
The perimeter of the garden is marked off with a rustic trellis, which provides structure for climbing pole bean plants. Other nearby edibles include blueberries, raspberries, kale, carrots, sweet peas, tomatoes, and cucumbers.

PULL IT TOGETHER

Lady's-mantle
These blossoms should be snipped off before they mature to keep this prolific self-sower in check. Afternoon shade will help prevent leaf scorch.

Allium
These come in shades of white, blue, yellow, red, and purple. Oniony leaves resist pests; flowers can be pungent or sweet, depending on variety.

Bleeding heart
This woodland classic blooms in late spring, with arching rows of flowers rising above delicate fernlike foliage. It's short-lived in mild-winter climates.

Russian sage
It stands tall, up to 4 feet. The lilac-blue sun worshipper, which is neither Russian nor sage but instead a Himalayan mint, yields four months of flowering.

Flowering tobacco
This plant lends color and fragrance to beds and borders all summer long. Although technically a perennial, it can be grown almost anywhere as an annual.

Switch grass
Billowing over a low rock wall, switch grass is green in the summer, gold in fall. It adds fine-textured mass to the garden, and moves gently in the breeze.

Check with your local nursery to see what plants thrive in your area.

GRAB A…
wheelbarrow

It's wise to keep a wheelbarrow, the workhorse of any garden, at the ready for easily toting soil, gravel, weeds, or plants. Before you're tempted to go for a super roomy one, keep in mind that the larger it is, the heavier and harder to handle it may be. Wheelbarrows are also ideal because they fit easily in narrow spaces.

ADD A…
bench

From a teak English garden style to a brightly painted charmer, a bench instantly dresses up any garden space (not to mention providing a spot to soak in the scenery). They're beautiful in wood, metal, concrete, or even rough-hewn stones, so position one next to your most fragrant blooms.

PULL UP…
Adirondack chairs

After weeding and pruning, what's better than plopping into this comfy classic, with a handy arm rest wide enough to hold a refreshing lemonade? For placement outside in the garden, consider synthetic, weather-resistant versions.

9
ROMANTIC GARDENS

Delicate roses, verdant arbors, a table set for two by the sea—that's what romantic gardens are made of. And plenty more, it turns out, as you turn the following pages to encounter the gorgeous plantings and panoramic views from these lovingly tended spaces that bring out the eternal romantic in us.

all tiered up

Divided into two terraces, this Maine garden's mix of annuals and perennials means there's always something in bloom—and beckoning oceanfront spaces in which to entertain.

HIGH AND LOW
This hillside garden is split into upper and lower levels, which are then broken up into more intimate pockets framed by hedges and colorful beds. The upper terrace provides a comfortable setting for cool evenings, while the lower, more exposed level is a prime spot for lobster bakes on the beach.

WIDE-OPEN SPACES
Marked off by dense shrubs and colorful borders, spacious mowed lawns are a soothing visual counterpoint to densely layered beds and create quiet spots for gathering with friends or unwinding alone.

SIDE BY SIDE
In both the upper and lower tiered beds, as well as in borders planted along the stone walls surrounding the garden, ornamental grasses serve as a hardy green foil for colorful blooms in magenta, orange-red, and yellow.

SPACED OUT

From the perch on the porch, the divided spaces of this garden unfold one by one. The areas open up to each other, making them well suited for parties, where guests can wander from mingling zones to dining areas to viewing spots.

SIGN LANGUAGE

A simple white gate with a painted sign that reads "My Beloved's Garden" opens to a grassy landing; the arbor then leads to the rocky beach below, where the home-owners enjoy casual meals at the picnic table.

PICTURE-PERFECT VIEWS

A mix of hardscapes and plantings, like the vine-covered arbor and the hedgerows, break up the garden's pan-oramic ocean views into telescoped perspectives that yield vistas of outlying islands, wildlife, and boats.

happy hillside

With a mix of lush green shrubs, ornamental grasses, sprays of colorful flowers, and climbing roses, this sloped garden in Los Angeles projects abundant cheer—nearly spilling it into the street— without appearing unkempt or overgrown.

A NATURAL LOOK
Up close, the hillside bed's combination of dense plantings looks almost random or haphazard. Take a step back, however, and the whole picture reveals a careful balance of color and texture without losing the wild, natural look.

STREETSIDE SPLENDOR
Planting additional shrubs, grasses, and flowers on the other side of the sidewalk not only expands the garden's merriment but also extends a warm welcome to visitors and passersby.

MAGICAL MIX
Delicate sweet peas, silky soft grasses, and spiky pride of Madeira have benefits beyond their beauty. Choosing a variety of plants instead of one uniform type is a smart way to disguise weeds and plant imperfections, which means less maintenance.

HIGH CLIMBERS
Against the Cape Cod-style house's dark gray shingles, pretty pink Eden Climber roses trained along the walls lend lots of romantic softness.

FANTASTIC FRAGRANCE
Sweet-smelling jasmine and roses are cleverly placed on either side of an entrance. Their fresh scents and beautiful blooms create an aromatic welcome.

SETTING LIMITS
Rather than letting flowering vines take over, limit them to just a few architectural features, like columns, pergolas, and railings.

beauty by the sea

A 4-acre home along the Maine coast lends itself to secret gardens and wonderful flower-filled paths.

HEDGE FIND
Lined with boxwood hedges, this walled-off space creates an intimate setting for reading, reflecting, or catching up with a friend before opening up to the large garden's big water views.

FRUITFUL THOUGHT
Training the branches of the espaliered pear and apple trees horizontally along the fence optimizes their fruit production by maximizing their sunlight exposure.

ROOM WITH A VIEW
The best gardens hold destinations. Here, it's a gazebo perched at garden's edge. Overlooking the sea, it's an inviting spot for weather-watching, garden planning, and alfresco meals on warm summer days—and a dry retreat during rain showers.

STANDING GUARD
Gardens require protection from strong winds and hungry animals. A dense line of hickory trees offers shelter from ocean gusts, while nearly invisible wire fencing keeps pests at bay.

A SOFTER SIDE
The climbing rose-covered moon gate is a lush entry to a colorful garden.

WILD AND WONDERFUL
At the edge of the garden along the shore, informal grasses with mowed walkways provide untamed contrast to the garden's more manicured sections.

PULL IT TOGETHER

soft plants

A mix of colorful blooms and verdant greenery ensures something's always peaking, keeping the charm of a romantic garden going all year.

'Flirt' Asiatic lily (yellow) and 'Rozanne' geranium (blue)
The lily is very hardy and easy to grow (especially in Northern gardens), as long as it's planted in soil that drains well. The geranium is pest- and disease-resistant and blooms throughout the summer with minimal care.

Oriental poppy
This 30-inch perennial's huge flowers come in shades of white, pink, red, mauve, and orange, with heavy bloom in late spring. These make good cut flowers if you sear cut stem ends with a flame before putting them in water.

Poppy (orange) and yarrow (yellow)
Welsh poppy, a perennial, grows 2 feet high, blooms all summer in mild climates, and prefers full sun. Yarrow, also a perennial, is often planted as a companion to other plants because it attracts good predatory insects, like wasps, and repels bad ones.

Delphinium
This is an excellent cutting flower for arrangements. When planted in well-drained soil, the spiky plant with bright blue blooms flourishes in full sun or light shade.

Dwarf conifers
Grown in a hypertufa container, these contrasting dwarf conifers thrive on a windowsill. There are hundreds of kinds; start with dwarf hinoki cypress and trailing juniper.

Westerland rose
This salmon-colored rose that grows well along fences or arbors is disease- and pest-resistant and boasts a strong, fruity scent.

Check with your local nursery to see what plants thrive in your area.

ADD AN …
arbor

A sweet spot in any garden, arbors are an easy and inviting way to add architecture to outdoor spaces. Heavy with climbing roses and flowering vines, these structures conjure images of fairy-tale gardens. Used to establish an entrance or as a transition to a new section of the garden, arbors are pretty and functional, lending framework, height, and interest to a space.

TRY A…
gate

A gate is to a garden what a front door is to a home—it's the first thing guests see, and an opportunity to make a lasting first impression. A white picket-style gate fits well in a romantic garden, evoking a sense of charm and simplicity. For a more rustic look, choose one crafted from natural materials that will blend into the landscape. Opt for an iron gate with decorative scrolls for a more formal garden space. Take cues from your home when settling on a style—you want the two to make sense together.

FINISH WITH …
sculptural details

Think of garden artwork as icing on the cake. Small, decorative finials topping gateposts add a touch of personality. Larger gardens often feature statuary, making the space an outdoor gallery. Keep the scale of your garden in mind when shopping for decorative elements. The pieces should complement, not overshadow, the living things that make a garden so lovely.

10

EXOTIC GARDENS

You don't have to live in a tropical spot to channel its spirit and look. The creative landscapes in this chapter take on an exotic flair in different ways, from wild, dense, and dramatic to more tailored, airy, and modern. Here, you'll get great ideas for creating a green space that provides a relaxing, escape-from-it-all vacation vibe the whole year through.

jungle fever

A landscape architect designed this South Florida garden with verdant plantings in an array of sizes, shapes, and textures—plus a few pops of intense color—for a fun island feel.

LAYER FOR LUSHNESS
A mix of towering palms, midsize perennials like red-orange bromeliads, and low-lying ground cover creates a natural look that's easy to maintain.

STUNNING SHADES
You don't have to have a bevy of blooms—here, interest comes in the many shades of green, from deep to nearly neon.

BIG BANG
Big-leafed plants can set a tropical tone even in temperate climates. Widely adapted choices include such plants as hardy palms and bananas, gunneras, bear's breech, and Japanese aralia.

CHEERFUL GREETING
Reminiscent of island resort entries, these hot pink bougainvilleas offer a warm welcome. To get a similar effect in frost-prone coastal climates, plant a hardy passion flower, jasmine, honeysuckle—or even a tender golden trumpet grown as an annual.

PRIMITIVE PATH
With its uneven surface, meandering direction, and hand-laid nature, this stone path has a primitive feel characteristic of one that cuts through a tropical jungle. Get the same effect for less by sprinkling coarse rock salt over wet concrete pavers and pressing it into the surface.

NATIVE ROCK
Incorporate stone that's natural to your area, such as Florida's limestone or key stone. Often found in tropical landscapes, black river rock can also be used as ground cover.

modern courtyard

Unexpected elements—such as a hint of hot pink and antique cobblestones—keep this mostly green, compact garden in Southern California dramatic and lively.

GEOMETRY LESSON
Manicured shrubs like these coiffed globe box-woods provide a little order in the wild, as well as subtle sophistication.

TWO-TONED
Sticking with mostly green plantings keeps the mood Zen in this contained garden. A bold hot pink bougainvillea elevates the color in this other-wise flowerless garden.

WATER FEATURE
A pair of squared-off lily ponds bring a peaceful, reflective quality to the serene space.

Steal This Idea
Position lanterns strategically to illuminate steps wherever they appear in your outdoor space.

THE HIGH ROAD
Pairs of Medjool palm trees and potted bamboo plants rise above the rest of the garden like exclamation points around entries to the walkway and house. Underplantings such as rosemary and lavender offer fragrant contrast.

OLD-WORLD STYLE
Salvaged European cobblestones paving the courtyard and driveway infuse a touch of patina to the garden's sleek aesthetic.

OPPOSITES ATTRACT
Sculptural aged urns mingle with square contemporary planters, providing a balance of old and new.

PULL IT TOGETHER

TRY THESE…
colorful plants
A mix of bright blooms, native plants, and adaptable tropical perennials give your garden space lush drama and exotic charm.

Cineraria
This shade-tolerant perennial is usually grown as a cool-season annual. It flowers from late winter through early summer and comes in a variety of colors—from pinks and blues to whites and purples—often with contrasting centers.

Calla
This easy-to-grow perennial prefers moisture and morning sun. The trumpet-shaped flowers bloom in winter and early spring and are popular for cut-flower arrangements. It also makes a good potted patio or deck plant.

New Zealand flax
Maturing into big clumps of swordlike leaves, these subtropical perennials do best in mild climates. In the warmer part of their range, they produce reddish tubular flowers loved by hummingbirds. Evergreen most places, these freeze back when temperatures reach the teens. Compact forms available.

Lily-of-the-Nile
Loved for big clusters of beguiling blue or white flowers that rise above clumps of strap-shaped leaves, these low-care perennials are equally effective in the ground and in containers. They come in deciduous and evergreen forms. All kinds do best in warm, sunny locations.

Strawberry geranium
Neither strawberry nor geranium, this hard perennial saxifrage thrives in shade, producing a constellation of pointy white flowers in late summer and fall. Roundish, begonia-like leaves spread by runners. Needs good drainage.

Daylily
Offered in shades of red, orange, pink, yellow, and purple, daylily flowers rise above clumps of sword-shaped foliage in mid to late spring. Each bloom lasts just a day, but they are abundant. Grow deciduous kinds in cold-winter climates, evergreen types where it's warmer. Full sun.

Check with your local nursery to see what plants thrive in your area.

SET UP A...
fire pit

It'll be your favorite new hot spot—right at home. Options vary from compact portables to big built-ins, but regardless of the type, it's where guests will gravitate—and it's a way to enjoy your outdoor space even in chilly weather. Types great at standing up to the elements include stainless steel and powder-coated copper.

ADD A...
birdbath

Your options are endless, from enamel to stone to sea glass, and pedestal to hanging. Or spring for a fabulous sculptural fountain to enjoy the serene sound of running water for a tranquil escape.

GET A...
gazing ball

They've been looking lovely in gardens for centuries. In glass, mirrored stainless steel, mosaic patterns, and more, these lawn ornaments draw you in and reflect the pleasures of the garden.

11
CONTAINER GARDENS

They're the ultimate garden problem solver: Container gardens require little space and maintenance, and with proper soil, drainage, exposure, and nourishment, you can grow almost anything in a container, from flowering plants to edible gardens. Whether your garden spans several acres or several windowsills, these ideas will help you create beautiful—and manageable— solutions for all kinds of challenges.

succulent containers

Containerized succulent arrangements change as they grow, but ever so slowly. The "picture" you create now can hold up for two or three years; then just repot and create a new living mosaic.

SEA SALT
Potted succulents are a great choice for a beach house deck or patio—their hardy leaves stand up to both sun and salt, plus they're so low-maintenance that there's plenty of time for play.

EASY DOES IT
The camels of container plants, succulents thrive on less than half the water of other ornamentals. Over-watering causes roots to rot and tops to die.

DRAINY DAY
Succulents demand plenty of sun and excellent drainage, so plant in a container with a hole in the bottom and a free-draining potting mix. Water just enough that plants don't become dull and wrinkled.

herbs & edibles containers

Fragrant herbs and fresh edibles like leafy greens and beans are easy to maintain when planted in containers—and a cooking staple to stash within reach just outside your kitchen door.

HAPPY TOGETHER
Billowy bronze fennel stands upright in the back, supporting scarlet runner bean vines; red leaf lettuce and green bok choy fill the rest of the container, while purple-flowered chives grow in the foreground.

SUN SEEKERS
Bathed in full-on sunshine, three big containers produce enough patty pan squash, tomatoes, and lemon cucumbers to supply fresh veggies all summer long.

GROWTH SPURT
The more you pick, the more you'll get, so pluck away! Edibles and herbs can also thrive in a container with annuals or perennials, as long as they have the same requirements for light and water.

shade containers

Spice up the cooler spots around your garden with artful arrangements of shade-loving plants.

SHADY LADIES
Angel-wing begonia, fuchsia 'Autumnale,' and roundleaf fern all thrive in the shade and are a stunning trio for a porch.

RULE OF THUMB
When planting a container garden, remember this trifecta: thriller, spiller, filler. Start with a taller focal point (the thriller), then add the spiller, which typically falls over the side of the pot. The filler should nestle in between.

HOLD EVERYTHING
To complement the design of the house behind them, the owners placed three antiquated terra-cotta pots containing ferns and variegated ground ivy on a permeable pea gravel surface. All grow in the shelter of a trident maple that acts as a centerpiece for the arrangement.

planning

More than any other exterior feature, paint colors set the tone for the entire home. From exotic brights and sandy whites to classic nautical combos and beachy neutrals, there's a coastal palette to suit every look—and that's just the beginning of the helpful information in this chapter. We also include handy tips for freshening up and maintaining your outdoor spaces all year long, as well as design worksheets to help you organize thoughts and ideas as you plan your personal oasis. Let the following pages help you translate the inspiration from the previous chapters into action!

seaside classics

SEA CAPTAIN CHIC

SIDING:

a true medium gray that softens the transition from stark white to black

TRIM:

a cool white with blue undertones— the perfect match for gray

DOOR:

a dark gray-black that gives definition without creating too much contrast

Inspired by long summer days spent on docks, boats, and beaches along America's coastlines, these time-honored combinations include nautical blues and whites with neutral grays and occasional red accents. If you're drawn to sporty stripes and traditional, tailored style, these paint picks are perfect for you.

To replicate these combos, take these samples to your local paint store to find a match.

YACHT CLUB

SIDING:

a dark navy warmed with just a touch of green

TRIM:

an off-white that doesn't feel cold but works well with blues

DOOR:

a little pop of an intense tomato red shade is all it takes to liven up a predictable scheme

daring brights

TROPICAL PUNCH

SIDING:
a tangy light green that's vibrant without overpowering the palette

DOOR:
a saturated shade that feels as pure as the sea

WINDOWS AND ACCENTS:
an upbeat, fuchsia shade inspired by island flowers and frozen strawberry daquiris

Beach locales like the Caribbean or the Florida Keys are known for their colorful crowds and laid-back aesthetics. If your version of a dream beach vacation includes either a trip to the shore in a convertible with the top down and the music blaring, or looking out at lush island vegetation with a frozen drink in your hand, consider setting a similar relaxed, carefree vibe at home with some of these bright hues.

CITRUS SQUEEZE

SIDING:
a soft, creamy yellow that's a colorful backdrop for more intense shades

TRIM:
an off-white shade with the faintest hint of yellow

SHUTTERS AND PORCH FLOOR:
a pretty turquoise blue that looks right at home in any seaside abode

natural neutrals

HARBOR MIST

SIDING:
a neutral, crowd-pleasing gray that works anywhere with almost anything

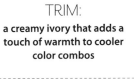

TRIM:
a creamy ivory that adds a touch of warmth to cooler color combos

DOOR:
a deep blue that's best used for accents, like shutters or doors

There's something magnetically captivating about the raw and untamed quality of the coast—and the stormy blue, earthy green, and weathered gray-brown colors that characterize it. Bring home some of that rustic beauty with these groupings inspired by the natural landscape.

BEACH BOUND

SIDING:
a cool, medium brown with gray undertones that give it a sophisticated, timeless feel

TRIM:
an earthy red that, in small doses, energizes a more neutral scheme without overpowering it

SHUTTERS:
a verdant leafy green that freshens up taupes, grays, and browns

crisp combos

GREEK GETAWAY

SIDING:
with subtle pink undertones, this color brings to mind the stucco homes on Greek islands

TRIM:
a crisp, true white that works with everything

DOOR:
a crystal clear shade that, when used as an accent, will add just a touch of far-flung flair to any exterior

From crisp sails to sun-bleached seashells and sugary island sand, an array of white shades figures prominently into coastal color palettes. The range is so vast that there's an option to suit every style, setting, or accent color—like the standout hues shown here.

MODERN CABANA

SIDING:
a white with just the faintest touch of green, is a perfect backdrop for a manicured lawn or garden

TRIM AND SHUTTERS:
a true black that, in a high-gloss sheen, is a classic choice for exterior accents

DOOR:
just the right amount of peppy tang for cheerful accents, like front doors

entries & exteriors

measurements:

square footage: (length x width)

ideas I love:

my wish list:

other notes:

color swatches: (attach here)

porches & loggias

measurements:

square footage: (length x width)

ideas I love:

my wish list:

other notes:

color swatches: (attach here)

pavilions, pergolas & gazebos

measurements:

square footage: (length x width)

ideas I love:

my wish list:

other notes:

color swatches: (attach here)

kitchens, dining areas & bars

measurements:

square footage: (length x width)

ideas I love:

my wish list:

other notes:

color swatches: (attach here)

pools & cabanas

measurements: ....

square footage: .... (length x width)

ideas I love: ....

....

....

....

....

....

....

my wish list: ....

....

....

....

....

....

....

....

other notes: ....

....

....

color swatches: (attach here)

outdoor showers

measurements: ....

square footage: .... (length x width)

ideas I love: ....

....

....

....

....

....

....

my wish list: ....

....

....

....

....

....

....

....

other notes: ....

....

....

color swatches: (attach here)

patios, decks & docks

measurements:

square footage: _____ (length x width)

ideas I love:

my wish list:

other notes:

color swatches: (attach here)

gardens

measurements:

square footage: _____ (length x width)

ideas I love:

my wish list:

other notes:

color swatches: (attach here)

annual cleaning tips

OUTDOOR SURFACES

☐ **WOOD (OR COMPOSITE) STEPS, SIDING, AND DECKING**
Pressure wash these areas to tackle dirt and mildew. (You can rent pressure washers by the day from most home and garden centers.) Avoid tiled surfaces, which can loosen from the force.

☐ **CONCRETE WALLS, FLOORS, OR PATIOS**
Rid the surface of grimy buildup with a 10:1 solution of warm water and biodegradable all-purpose cleaner. (Environmentally safe cleaners are essential outside because there will be runoff that drains into your yard.) Leave on the mixture for 15 minutes, then scrub with a stiff broom, and rinse. For stains, add bleach to the solution—about 1 cup for a 10- by 10-foot patio.

☐ **STONE PATIOS**
After sweeping and weeding between pavers, apply the pressure washer, then treat the patio with a cleaner formulated for stone patios, and rinse thoroughly. Be sure to hose off any vegetation or furniture that may have been soaked by the cleaning mixture.

☐ **BRICK WALKWAYS AND PATIOS**
After weeding between bricks and sweeping with a stiff-bristle push broom, spray down with a hose, then mop with a mixture of equal parts warm water and an all-purpose cleaner.

☐ **TILE PATIOS**
Pour a solution of oxygen bleach and warm water on the patio (mixed per manufacturer's instructions), and allow it to penetrate for 15 minutes. Scrub the tile with a nylon brush, focusing on the grout, then rinse with a hose.

☐ **TEAK DECKS**
Wet down teak decks with a hose, then mop with a solution of 1 gallon of water mixed with 1 cup of ammonia. Scrub any tough stains with a nonabrasive scrubbing pad, then allow the cleaning solution to sit for up to 20 minutes. Rinse thoroughly.

OUTDOOR FURNISHINGS

☐ **TEAK FURNITURE**
Clean furniture with a soft brush. Scrub gently with a 50/50 mixture of warm water and mild soap. Apply a teak sealer on an annual basis for added protection.

☐ **WOOD AND WICKER FURNITURE**
Clean with a soft brush and mild dish soap. (Anything harsher could damage the surface.) Wipe clean with a damp cloth.

☐ **POWDER-COATED ALUMINUM FURNITURE**
Wipe down with a soft kitchen sponge and soapy water. Don't scrub; if the finish wears off, the surface will become more vulnerable to the elements and likely corrode over time.

☐ **WROUGHT IRON**
Remove algae buildup from furniture or railings with a brush and a strong disinfectant.

☐ **WINDOWS**
Wipe down with a vinegar-soaked sponge to remove residue from environmental factors such as salt spray.

☐ **LIGHT FIXTURES**
Wipe with a soft, damp microfiber cloth. Avoid chemical cleaners, which leave a filmy coating.

☐ **OUTDOOR CUSHION COVERS AND UMBRELLAS**
Apply an environmentally safe cleaner, then wipe down with a damp sponge. Prop them in the sun to dry.

resources

ENTRIES & EXTERIORS

Refined Welcome, page 14
Architect Bobby McAlpine, McAlpine Tankersley and McAlpine;
mcalpinetankersley.com

Island Aloha, page 16
Designer Barry Dixon; **barrydixon.com**

California Cool, page 20
Designer Tim Clarke, Tim Clarke, Inc;
timclarkeinc.com

Rustic Hideaway, page 24
Designer Sue White, White Design;
suewhitedesign.com

PORCHES & LOGGIAS

Opener, page 28 top right
Designer Lee Ann Thornton,
Thornton Designs;
leeannthornton.com

Opener, page 28 bottom left
Designer Todd Alexander
Romano; **toddalexanderromano.com**

Polished Ease, page 30
Architect Robert A.M. Stern,
Robert A.M. Stern Architects;
ramsa.com

Bold Gesture, page 32
Designer William Diamond, Anthony
Baratta, LLC; **anthonybaratta.com**

Screen Saver, page 34
Designer Amanda Nisbet,
Amanda Nisbet Design;
amandanisbetdesign.com

Sleeping Beauty, page 36
Architect Robert A.M. Stern, Robert
A.M. Stern Architects; **ramsa.com**

Old World, page 42
Designer Susan Lapelle, Susan Lapelle
Interiors; 404/705-9695

Coastal Tradition, page 44
Designer Meg Braff, Meg Braff Interiors;
megbraff.com

PAVILIONS, PERGOLAS & GAZEBOS

Opener, page 48 top left
Designer Amanda Lindroth,
Lindroth Design;
amandalindroth.com

Opener, page 48 bottom right
Architect Clemens Bruns Schaub,
Clemens Bruns Schaub Architect &

Associates; **cbsarchs.com**; Designers
Ashley Waddell and Courtney Whatley,
Olivia O'Bryan, Inc.; **oliviaobryan.com**

Natural Wonder, page 50
Designer Meg Braff, Meg Braff Interiors;
megbraff.com

Soft Spot, page 52
Designer Barry Dixon; **barrydixon.com**

Louver's Lane, page 56
Architect Clemens Bruns Schaub, Clemens
Bruns Schaub Architect & Associates;
cbsarchs.com

Rustic Warmth, page 58
Architect Steve Hoedemaker,
Bosworth Hoedemaker;
bosworthhoedemaker.com

Four-Seasons Room, page 60
Architect Michael Imber and
Designer Marcus Mohon,
Mohon-Imber Interiors;
mohon-imber.com

KITCHENS, DINING AREAS & BARS

Opener, page 66 top left
Residential Designer Brian Carnes, BC
Architects; **bcarchitectsinc.com**

Opener, page 66 top right
Architect Clemens Bruns Schaub,
Clemens Bruns Schaub Architect &
Associates; **cbsarchs.com**; Designers
Ashley Waddell and Courtney Whatley,
Oliva O'Bryan, Inc.; **oliviaobryan.com**

Opener, page 66 bottom left
Designer Barry Dixon; **barrydixon.com**

Rock Solid, page 68
Designer Phillip Sides, Phillip Sides
Interior Design; 334/240-3333

Open Air, page 74
Architect John Kell, Kell Munoz
Architects; **kellmunoz.com**;
Architectural designer Jennifer Kell;
310/699-1601

Fine Dining, page 80
Designer Erika McPherson Powell,
Urban Grace Interiors;
urbangrace.com

Au naturel, p. 82
Designer Erin Curci; ecurci@road
runner.com; Landscape designer
Molly Wood; **mollywoodgarden
design.com**

POOLS & CABANAS

Opener, page 86 bottom right
Designer Barry Dixon; **barrydixon.com**

Courtyard Paradise, page 88
Designer Erika McPherson Powell,
Urban Grace Interiors; **urbangrace.com**

Modern Gem, page 90
Project Designer Alisa Thiry, Redefine
Real Estate; alisathiry@yahoo.co.uk

Woodland Sanctuary, page 92
Architect Marshall Perrow; 253/627-
4765; Landscape architect Dennis
Harris, White Rabbit Landscaping;
206/724-7223

Palm Spring, page 96
Architect Clemens Bruns Schaub,
Clemens Bruns Schaub Architect
& Associates; **cbsarchs.com**

OUTDOOR SHOWERS

Opener, page 104 top left
Architects Phil Regan and Jim
Cappuccino, Hutker Architects, Inc.;
hutkerarchitects.com

Opener, page 104 bottom right
Architecture Butler Armsden
Architects; **butlerarmsden.com**

Minimalist Spa, page 108
Architectural Eric Olsen; 714/771-8400;
Interior designers Heidi Bonesteel
and Michelle Trout;
bonesteeltrouthall.com

Tropical Hideaway, page 110
Landscape designer Vickie Cardaro,
Buttercup Design Group; **buttercup
designgroup.com**; Designer Jonathan
Adler; **jonathanadler.com**

Double Duty, p. 112
Architect Gerry Cowart, Cowart
Coleman Group; cowartgroup.com;
Interior designer Jane Coslick, Jane
Coslick Designs & Restorations;
janecoslick.com

Simply Modern, page 114
Architect Ward Welch, CWB Architects;
cwbarchitects.com; Architect Paul
Rice, Paul Rice Architecture;
paulricearchitecture.com

PATIOS, DECKS & DOCKS

Classic Charm, page 120
Designer John Bjornen, Bjornen
Design; **bjornendesign.com**

Organic Refuge, page 122
Designer Angie Hranowsky;
angiehranowsky.com

Modern Comfort, page 124
Designer Erin Curci; ecurci@road
runner.com; Landscape designer
Molly Wood; **mollywoodgarden
design.com**

Camp Ground, page 126
Designer April Tidey; **apriltidey.com**

Rooftop Retreat, page 128
Architect Bruce Bolander;
brucebolander.com

Sun Seeker, page 132
Designer Amanda Lindroth, Lindroth
Design; **amandalindroth.com**

CLASSIC GARDENS

Opposites Attract, page 140
Garden Designer: Gary Ratway,
Integrated Designs; 707/937-1235

Raised Expectations, page 148
Garden Designer: S.A. Hatch
Landscapes and Gardens;
207/734-6407

ROMANTIC GARDENS

Happy Hillside, page 160
Garden designer: Sabine Hoppner,
Water's Edge Gardening;
watersedge@sbcglobal.net

EXOTIC GARDENS

Jungle Fever, page 172
Garden Designer: Raymond Jungles,
Raymond Jungles, Inc.;
raymondjungles.com

Modern Courtyard, page 176
Garden designer: Scott Shrader, Scott
Shrader Design; **shraderdesign.com**

index